0048242

D1299822

WITHDRAWN

DATE DUE	
ILL 9-5-90	
SEP 2 6 1990	
DEC 1 6 1991	
FEB 1 9 1992	
OCT 1 2 1992	
OCT 2 7 1993	
APR 0 3 1995	
MAY 0 2 1995	
OCT 1 7 1997	

BRODART, INC.   Cat. No. 23-221

THE BUSINESS OF LISTENING

A Practical Guide to Effective Listening

Diane Bone

CRISP PUBLICATIONS, INC.
Los Altos, California

THE BUSINESS OF LISTENING

A Practical Guide to Effective Listening

Diane Bone

CREDITS
Editor: **Michael Crisp**
Designer: **Carol Harris**
Typesetting: **Interface Studio**
Cover Design: **Carol Harris**
Artwork: **Ralph Mapson**

Copyright © 1988 by Crisp Publications, Inc.
Printed in the United States of America

Crisp books are distributed in Canada by Reid Publishing, Ltd., P.O. Box 7267, Oakville, Ontario, Canada L6J 6L6.

In Australia by Prime Learning Australia, Rochedale South, 7 Deputor Street, Brisbane, Queensland.

And in New Zealand by Prime Learning Pacific, 18 Gibbons Road, Weymouth, Auckland.

Library of Congress Catalog Card Number 87-72485
Bone, Diane
The Business of Listening
ISBN 0-931961-34-3

ABOUT THIS BOOK

THE BUSINESS OF LISTENING is not like most books. It stands out from other self-help books in an important way. It's not a book to read—it's a book to *use*. The unique "self-paced" format of this book and the many worksheets, encourage the reader to get involved and, try some new ideas immediately.

Using the simple yet sound techniques presented can make a dramatic change in one's ability to listen effectively.

THE BUSINESS OF LISTENING (and other books listed on page 67) can be used effectively in a number of ways. Here are some possibilities:

—**Individual Study.** Because the book is self-instructional, all that is needed is a quiet place, some time and a pencil. By completing the activities and exercises, a reader should not only receive valuable feedback, but also practical steps for self-improvement.

—**Workshops and Seminars.** The book is ideal for assigned reading prior to a workshop or seminar. With the basics in hand, the quality of the participation will improve, and more time can be spent on concept extensions and applications during the program. The book is also effective when it is distributed at the beginning of a session, and particpants "work through" the contents.

—**Remote Location Training.** Books can be sent to those not able to attend "home office" training sessions.

There are several other possibilities that depend on the objectives, program or ideas of the user.

One thing for sure, even after it has been read, this book will be looked at—and thought about—again and again.

PREFACE

If you want to improve your ability to listen effectively in your business and personal life, this book is for you. Most of us are not good listeners. While at work, we normally listen at about 25% of our listening capacity. Most of us *think* we are good listeners, and that overconfidence may be the reason for our downfall. Even if we devote full concentration to listening we cannot listen at 100% efficiency for very long. And at 100% efficiency, the message we are listening to must be important enough to sustain our attention.

Humans, listen more than anything else, except breathe. Carefully reading this book will help you learn to listen better, on the job and at home. Before good listening can happen you must want to be a good listener. Whether you are a secretary, an account executive, a programmer or a project manager, you can improve your listening if you have the desire, the interest, a high level of concentration, self-discipline and a positive attitude.

This book will provide you with important listening know-how. It is a self-study introduction to the basic skills you need to become a better listener. It will provide many helpful suggestions for incorporating more effective listening skills into your business day. Listening styles and motivation are highly individual, so there is no claim as to how much your listening skills will improve. We offer many suggestions for improvement, along with some motivation to help you make constructive changes in your listening style. After completing THE BUSINESS OF LISTENING, you can practice your new-found listening awareness on business associates, family and friends.

Each section in this book provides insightful information, useful tips and practical guidelines for upgrading your skills. These are the *why, what,* and *how* of listening. Each section contains activities called ''Listening Labs'' as well as case studies and check lists. They provide ''hands on'' reinforcements and illustrations for the key principles of the book.

Section I provides answers to the important question, ''Why should I become a better listener?''

Section II describes how good listeners process information and reach higher levels of listening expertise.

Section III individual listening styles are identified as barriers or bridges to communication.

Section IV contains pencil exercises to help you define your listening strengths and weaknesses.

Section V provides ten tips to reinforce your listening strengths, control your weaknesses, and reach new levels of listening effectiveness.

Plan to find three ideas from this book to begin practicing immediately. Use *The Business of Listening* as a reference and challenge yourself to practice until you have mastered each new skill. Remember: practice, properly done, does not make perfect, it makes permanent. Listening well will help you function more effectively in both your business *and* personal life. So pick up your pencil, tune up your ears, and turn to Section I.

Happy Listening!

Diane Bone

Diane Bone

SOME IMPORTANT OBJECTIVES FOR THE READER

Objectives give us a sense of direction; a definition of what we plan to accomplish; and a sense of fulfillment when they are achieved. Check the objectives that are important to you. This book will help you achieve them.

By completing this book, I plan to:

☐ Learn the basics of effective listening skills.

☐ Learn to recognize good listening behaviors and incorporate them into my daily activities.

☐ Understand the impact of good listening skills on productivity.

☐ Learn to correct problems caused by poor listening habits and systematically change them into permanent good habits.

CONTENTS

THE BUSINESS OF LISTENING

In Business...

To listen effectively is to reach a clarity of understanding

To understand clearly is to respond appropriately

To respond appropriately is to enhance communication

To enhance communication is to support cooperation

To support cooperation is to improve morale

To improve morale is to increase job commitment

To increase job commitment is to focus on productivity

Listening is Good Business

SECTION I:
WHY SHOULD YOU (OR ANYONE) LISTEN?

What's In It For Me?

At least half of all communication time is spent listening. Experts in a dozen studies have verified that we listen more than any other activity, except breathing. Listening is the ''receiving'' part of communication. Listening is:

1) Receiving information through your ears (and eyes)

2) Giving meaning to that information

3) Deciding what you think (or feel) about that information

and,   4) Responding to what you hear.

Much of our listening is work related. We spend countless hours of our working life involved in listening related activities. Following is a partial list of work-related activities which involve listening. Check those which apply to you.

_____ attending meetings, briefings and lectures

_____ personal counseling (one-on-one)

_____ giving instructions

_____ receiving instructions

_____ interviewing others

_____ making decisions based on verbal information

_____ selling or marketing a product or service

_____ managing others

_____ helping clients

_____ servicing other groups or departments

_____ using the telephone

WHY SHOULD YOU (OR ANYONE) LISTEN?
(Continued)

If you are like most people, you checked most of the activities on the previous page. What other work-related activities can you think of that involve listening?

_____

_____

_____

_____

_____

What is the business of listening? More important, what's in it for you? Check those items with which you agree:

Listening effectively can:

☐ Increase your income.

☐ Improve your company's profits.

☐ Make you more promotable.

☐ Increase your job satisfaction.

☐ Improve your ability to solve problems.

☐ Keep you aware of what is going on in your organization.

BENEFITS OF GOOD LISTENING

THE BENEFITS OF LISTENING—A QUIZ

Read each of the following statements. Determine which are true and which are false about the benefits that good listening can bring about in business relationships. Check your answers with those of the author at the bottom of the page.

True or false

____ 1. Skill in listening improves your self confidence.

____ 2. People like you when you listen to them.

____ 3. Good listeners are usually more efficient in completing their work.

____ 4. What you create with good listening is flexibility in settling disagreements.

____ 5. Intelligent responses are easier when you listen.

____ 6. More decisions are made by "shooting from the hip" than by listening to the opinions of others.

____ 7. Learning to listen to clients helps you respond more quickly to their needs.

____ 8. Few good listeners are promoted to top management positions.

____ 9. Good listeners are not often embarrassed by unnecessary mistakes.

____ 10. Handling distractions is difficult for good listeners.

ANSWERS: 1.T 2.T 3.T 4.T 5.T 6.F (Committees, meetings and informal networks are strong evidence that most decisions are made by groups.) **7.T 8.F** (Most surveys rank listening as one of the three most important skills of top managers.) **9.T 10.F** (Good listeners know how to control distractions by eliminating or ignoring them.)

WHY SHOULD YOU (OR ANYONE) LISTEN? (Continued)

Organizations rely heavily upon listening as an important productivity tool. They need people who have good listening communication skills. Those who know how to listen can:

* Better understand problems

* Sustain attention

* Retain information

* Improve working relationships

BUSINESS THRIVES WHEN EMPLOYEES LISTEN

WHY SHOULD YOU (OR ANYONE) LISTEN? (Continued)

Asleep at the Switch: The Costs of Lazy Listening

Most of us are not good listeners. We listen at about 25% of our potential, which means we *ignore, forget, distort* or *misunderstand* 75% of what we hear. Hard to believe perhaps, but true. Such lazy listening habits can be very costly—both to our business and to ourselves.

Paul Leet of the Sperry Corporation recently stated: "Poor listening is one of the most significant problems facing business today. Business relies on clear communication. When communication breaks down, costly mistakes are made. Organizations pay for mistakes caused by poor listening with lower profits, and consumers pay for the same mistakes with higher prices."

Lazy listening is a hidden cost of doing business. Suppose you were employed by a large international company with 10,000 employees. If each person in the company made one $100 error each year because of poor listening, the company would lose a million dollars. This loss would be especially bad news if your company had a profit sharing plan or was forced to lay off workers due to poor earnings.

The following examples are true stories of the costs of lazy listening.

---

1 A sales manager for a large company asked his accounting department how he could charge off a $100,000 error caused by a dispatcher who routed a fleet of drivers to deliver building material to the wrong state. The dispatcher heard the city (Portland) but not the state (Maine). The result was eight trucks 3,000 miles off coast in Portland, Oregon. How could this problem have been avoided?

WHY SHOULD YOU (OR ANYONE) LISTEN?
(Continued)

2. Three computer sales representatives from different companies presented their products to a historian who had special application needs. The historian was a dealer in rare manuscripts and explained to each sales representative what computer functions were required. Two of the sales representatives did not listen and presented products that were inappropriate. The third understood what the historian wanted and she got the order. The manuscript dealer was impressed with only one thing, and it wasn't the hardware because he didn't know much about computers. He did know that two people didn't listen and the third did. He bought his computer from the person who listened. What was the cost to the other two companies?

3 Linda recently cut short a business trip to attend an important investment dinner meeting with her husband. She hurried from the airport, dressed for dinner and met her husband at the restaurant. An hour and a half later their financial advisor had not arrived. A phone call deduced they were at the right restaurant, but on the wrong night. The dinner was rescheduled, but Linda sacrificed profitable business she would have closed had she kept her original trip schedule. How can Linda avoid this problem in the future?

WHY SHOULD WE LISTEN?

Why should we listen? What are the advantages of overcoming lazy listening habits and changing unproductive ways of listening? List as many reasons as you can think of in the space below. Place a ☑ next to those that are most important to you. Then turn the page and read "Fifty Reasons to Become a Better Listener." Check any you would like to add to your list.

REASONS FOR ME TO BECOME A BETTER LISTENER

FIFTY PERFECTLY GOOD REASONS TO BECOME A BETTER LISTENER

1. To learn something.
2. To be entertained.
3. To understand a situation.
4. To get information.
5. To be courteous.
6. To be responsible.
7. To prevent accidents.
8. To be a team player.
9. To ask intelligent questions.
10. To improve confidence.
11. To protect freedom.
12. To find out people's needs.
13. To reach a productivity or sales quota.
14. To be valued and trusted.
15. To use money more wisely.
16. To be more efficient.
17. To make accurate evaluations.
18. To make comparisons.
19. To understand and be understood.
20. To analyze the speaker's purpose.
21. To develop a reputation of being a good listener.
22. To get the best value.
23. To improve discipline.
24. To enhance relationships.

25. To solve problems.

26. To show you care.

27. To satisfy curiosity.

28. To be safe.

29. To be a good lover.

30. To make intelligent decisions.

31. To prevent waste.

32. To make money.

33. To avoid embarrassment.

34. To stay out of trouble.

35. To save time.

36. To be a discriminating consumer.

37. To be a supportive friend.

38. To give an appropriate response.

39. To enjoy the sounds of nature.

40. To create ''win-win'' situations.

41. To control distractions.

42. To increase concentration.

43. To improve your vocabulary.

44. To build rapport.

45. To be prepared for sudden shifts in a speaker's topic or intention.

46. To be a better family member.

47. To settle disagreements.

48. To maintain a flexible attitude.

49. To improve your personality.

50. To use the gift of hearing.

THE JOY OF SMALL CHANGE

To improve the listening skills suggested in this book, we must be both motivated and educated. We must believe that each small change in lazy listening habits has value for us.

Change can be hard work. Setbacks sometimes occur just when we think we're making progress. To change our listening habits we must believe that the new skills we are gaining are worth the unproductive habits we are giving up. As you change your behavior to practice listening techniques presented in the pages ahead, the following suggestions will be helpful. To effectively change, it is recommended that you:

1. **Notice small changes.** Recognize your improvements and give yourself a pat on the back as they occur. Acknowledging improvements is a form of positive reinforcement.

2. **Keep a log of significant listening habit changes**—such as:

   * Enjoying a previously dull meeting.

   * Receiving positive responses from others.

   * Feeling good about not interrupting a co-worker at coffee.

3. **Acknowledge setbacks but do not give in to them.** Failure to learn from mistakes is the only real failure.

4. **Stay with it.** Unless you consciously work to improve your listening skills, you will find it easy to slip back into old (bad) habits.

SECTION II:
FOUR KEY ELEMENTS OF
GOOD LISTENING

HOW TO BE A GOOD LISTENER

Good listening is an active integrated communication skill that demands energy and know-how. It is purposeful, powerful and productive. To listen effectively we must *hear* and *select* information from the speaker, *give it meaning, determine how we feel about it*, and *respond,*—in a matter of seconds!

We must also understand the speaker's purpose in order to know how to listen most effectively. The speaker's purpose influences the way we listen and how we perceive what is said. The speaker and the listener must have the same purpose if communication is to be effective. Next time you are listening to someone, make sure you are aware what that person's purpose is. Is he or she:

_____ Entertaining you?

_____ Providing critical data?

_____ Persuading you?

_____ Sharing feelings?

_____ Making small talk?

On the following pages are the four key elements of the listening process. They describe what good listeners do to listen more effectively. After each element is a ''Listening Lab'' that contains suggestions and exercises to improve your listening skills.

FOUR KEY ELEMENTS OF GOOD LISTENING

KEY ELEMENT #1

HEAR THE MESSAGE

Our brain recognizes sound as it enters the ear. Other ''listening channels'' such as our eyes and our feelings seek confirmation of the message from the speaker's non-verbal feedback (body language) and tone of voice. Hearing is the *beginning* of the listening process. It is non-selective and involuntary. However, when you *choose* to listen, it is on purpose.

LISTENING IS VOLUNTARY

From the constant noise around us, we select what we want to listen to. This information moves from Short Term Memory (STM) to Long Term Memory (LTM). Short Term Memory is a ''holding pen'' for incoming signals from our five senses. In order to protect us from too much stimulation STM has a limited capacity and is easily disrupted. For instance, a mail clerk would not likely retain much information from a technical discussion about Data Transport Protocols because he/she would have no use for the message. The information would probably be held in STM for 1-30 seconds and then dismissed. If the information we hear is not recognized and selected for processing, it is dismissed from STM.

In a sense, we are pre-programmed. Our choices of what to listen to come from previous choices based on interests and needs. John enjoys investing in stocks and bonds, so he always has his ''ears open'' for tips on the market. Ellie ''tunes in'' whenever someone is discussing consumer rights. Ralph ''catches'' the football scores each Saturday in order to track his favorite teams. In other words, we choose what we want to listen to and often it is based on our past choices.

KEY ELEMENT #1 (Continued)

In order to listen to a speaker, we begin by *hearing* and *selecting* (paying attention to) oral messages, and accompanying non-verbal signals. When these messages are interesting or important, we pay attention to them.

We choose to listen because:

       a)   The message is important

       b)   We are interested

       c)   We feel like listening, or

       d)   We listened to this kind of information in the past

Sometimes, even when we choose to listen, anger, frustration, grief or hostility can act as "emotional cotton" in our ears. We tend to hear what we expect (or want) to hear, and filter out that which is not consistent with our feelings and attitudes. For example, Jennifer was on her way to lunch when her manager dropped a report on her desk and said he needed twenty sets of copies when he returned from lunch. Jennifer was upset because her friends were waiting and she assumed she had to make the copies. She did not hear her boss say after *his* lunch, which was an hour later than hers. She had ample time to make the copies after she returned from her lunch if she had listened carefully.

```
+------------------------------------------------+
|                                                |
|      THREE KEYS TO HEARING THE MESSAGE         |
|                                                |
|                                                |
|      PAY ATTENTION                             |
|                                                |
|      SELECT WHAT IS IMPORTANT                  |
|                                                |
|      RECOGNIZE EMOTIONAL MESSAGES              |
|                                                |
+------------------------------------------------+
```

LISTENING LAB FOR KEY ELEMENT #1
—HEAR THE MESSAGE

Exercise 1.

Sit quietly someplace where people are talking around you (hotel lobby, office corridor, restaurant, airport). Listen for about ten minutes and then write down what you heard, i.e., what people said, and other incidental sounds or noises. This activity should make you conscious of the many voices and sounds that bombard you daily. It should help remind you that listening begins with hearing but is a voluntary activity.

1. What did you hear?

2. How many sounds do you remember?

3. What sounds did you remember most easily?

4. Did your mind wander while you were listening?

5. Try the experiment again with your eyes closed and see if the results are the same. (You will notice how important your eyes are to listening.)

AUTHORS COMMENTS

1. We hear sounds constantly, but remember few.

2. We remember sounds that are important, interesting or unusual.

3. Same as #2.

4. All of us day dream frequently. We cannot remember what we did not hear.

5. People sometimes complain they can't listen as well when they are not wearing glasses because they cannot see speaker's non-verbal message.

LISTENING LAB FOR KEY ELEMENT #1
(Continued)

EXERCISE 2.

Listed below are some methods for improving listening at the ''hearing'' level. Write any others you can think of.

- Improving your listening vocabulary so that words and meanings are clear when you listen.

- Having your hearing checked.

- Asking for repetition or clarification.

- Overcoming a tendency to daydream.

- Eliminating distractions.

Others: • _____

• _____

• _____

• _____

• _____

FOUR KEY ELEMENTS OF GOOD LISTENING (Continued)

> ### KEY ELEMENT #2
> ### INTERPRET THE MESSAGE

Interpreting a speaker's message is coming to a mutual understanding of the speaker's meaning. Good listeners know that a match-up in meaning is a match-up in understanding. The word communication comes from the Latin root word **communis** which means "commonness", a commonness of understanding.

Listeners often experience problems at the interpreting level because no two people perceive things in the same way. Speakers do not always say exactly what they mean, or mean exactly what they say.

> ### WHAT IS THE DIFFERENCE?
> "When I look at you, time stands still."
> "You have a face that would stop a clock."

We probably do not interpret accurately in most listening situations. Listening is a complicated process. Speakers send messages to listeners both verbally and non-verbally. If Jim tells Rod, "You have to do something about the Doughty account," Rod must assign meaning to Jim's **words, filters, tone of voice,** and **non-verbal cues.**

WORDS Words themselves have little meaning. They are merely vehicles for the thoughts and feelings of the speaker. Words are not actual experiences, but a means of explaining experiences. It is people who give meaning to words.

INTERPRET THE MESSAGE (Continued)

FILTERS   Both listeners and speakers have filters which can help or hinder the interpreting process. These filters are in our brains "data base" and attach personal meaning to information as it is presented. Some examples of filters include the following: *Can you add others?*

memories	current attention span	language and vocabulary
perceptions	past experiences	needs and motives
biases	values	age
attitudes	knowledge and intelligence	sensory acuity
expectations	feelings	assumptions
emotional hotbuttons		

TONE OF VOICE   Most voices convey approximately 30% of the meaning of a message. Voices can be insistent, pleading, questioning, whining, demanding, etc. Tom speaks in a quiet monotone. Even though he is intelligent, his voice lacks conviction, and people don't take him seriously. What could Tom do with his voice to get people to listen to him?

NON-VERBAL CUES   A non-verbal cue, or body language, is a message sent by such things as a speaker's gestures, facial expressions, eyes and posture. Good listeners use their ears, eyes and intuition to interpret a speaker's non-verbal feedback. Non-verbal cues confirm or deny the message of the words and tone of voice. More than half of most human interaction is through non-verbal communication.

Good listeners who aren't sure of the speaker's meaning will ask for repetition or clarification (feedback).

"Is this what you mean when you say...?"

"This is how I interpret what you are saying...Am I correct?"

"I'm not sure I understand your meaning, could you be more specific?"

THREE KEYS TO INTERPRETING THE MESSAGE

SELF KNOWLEDGE

DESIRE TO UNDERSTAND

ASKING FOR CLARIFICATION

The Business of Listening

LISTENING LAB FOR KEY ELEMENT #2 —INTERPRET THE MESSAGE

Let us imagine you have just interviewed a young woman for an important sales position in your department. As she is leaving she remembers one last thing she wants you to know, and states: ''By the way, I graduated in the top 10% of my class.'' She then shakes your hand, thanks you for the interview and leaves. How would you interpret her statement? Following are some interpretations. Read these, then list five other possible interpretations of her statement.

> ''By the way, I graduated in the top 10% of my class.''

1. She is intelligent.

2. She is competitive.

3. The school was not academically challenging.

4. She studied constantly.

5. She was bragging.

6.

7.

8.

9.

10.

How would you clarify your interpretation?

See author's comments below.

Comments: Good listeners want to understand the speaker's meaning. They are aware of their own filters and those of the speaker, and they *ask questions* if they need clarification.

FOUR KEY ELEMENTS OF GOOD LISTENING (Continued)

KEY ELEMENT #3 **EVALUATE THE MESSAGE**

Good listeners make sure they have all of the key information before forming an opinion. They do not jump to conclusions based on a bias or incomplete information. They may agree or disagree with the speaker. Good listening does not mean automatic compliance. A good listener will weigh and analyze all of the evidence before reaching a final decision or making a written or verbal judgment.

> Diana is a member of a jury trying a felony case. As each attorney sifts through the evidence Diana listens carefully for validation of her opinions. She is careful not to jump to conclusions based on emotional testimony. At the conclusion of the trial Diana evaluates all of the evidence presented by both sides before making a statement about her decision. The jury foreman later thanked Diana for her valuable observations and objective comments.

We make conscientious evaluations when we make decisions based on *all* of the available information. We run into problems with evaluation when we think mechanically, or jump to conclusions. We must ask ourselves if we are listening *to* someone or listening *against* them. Are we *evaluating* or making a *value judgement*?

Evaluation is not required in every listening situation, therefore, we must also know our purpose for listening.

THREE KEYS TO EVALUATING THE MESSAGE ASK QUESTIONS ANALYZE THE EVIDENCE DON'T JUMP TO CONCLUSIONS

LISTENING LAB FOR KEY ELEMENT #3 —EVALUATE THE MESSAGE

We listen constantly to advertising on radio and television. How often do you stop to evaluate the slant or bias of advertisers who want us to buy their services or products? How often do you ask if the information is reasonable and logical? Following is a description of Adolph Hitler, as it may have been written by his press agent. Read the description as if you were listening to it, taking note of the press agent's built-in bias. Then answer the questions that follow.

> "Our leader had an unhappy childhood and little formal education. His father bitterly opposed his ambition to become an artist. Through self-education, he became the author of a book, that became a national bestseller. Obstacles do not discourage him. When others say, "that is not possible" he hurdles each barrier as it comes. He has built an active youth movement of selected young people. He is known throughout the world for his dynamic speeches. His closest associates say of him, "He accomplishes great deeds out of the passion of his will in order to create the kind of government he believes in."

1. How would you evaluate Hitler if you had not heard of him before you read this description?

2. Are any character flaws suggested in the description?

3. What suggestions does the press agent use to create a positive impression of Hitler?

4. How can this exercise help you evaluate information more carefully?

FOUR KEY ELEMENTS OF GOOD LISTENING (Continued)

> **KEY ELEMENT #4**
>
> **RESPOND TO THE MESSAGE**

Although a response may be considered a speaking rather than a listening role, it is critical to clear communication. The listener must let the speaker know by verbal and/or non-verbal feedback what was heard and how it was heard. Good listeners accept responsibility to provide feedback to the speaker in order to complete the communication process.

Good listeners have a strong desire to reach a common understanding. Responsible responses inform the speaker that:

1. The message was heard.
2. It was understood.
3. It was evaluated appropriately.

Several problems can occur in this key element. One is when no response occurs. If Karla asks Jack when the plans for the new office building will be available, and Jack simply looks at Karla without indicating that he heard her, he is not communicating effectively. Although silence can communicate, a blank stare is not a responsible response. Other problems include responses that are defensive, overly emotional, or inappropriate. If Jack had abruptly changed the subject, his response would have also been inappropriate. Finally, a confusing response (i.e. a double message) can occur when the verbal (words and tone of voice) and non-verbal (actions and body-language) are in conflict.

> **THREE KEYS TO RESPONDING TO THE MESSAGE**
>
> WANT TO REACH A COMMON UNDERSTANDING
>
> GIVE FEEDBACK VERBALLY AND/OR NON-VERBALLY
>
> AVOID CONFUSING MESSAGES

LISTENING LAB FOR KEY ELEMENT #4
—RESPOND TO THE MESSAGE.

Following are several possible responses in listening situations. Place a check next to those you think are important for good communication.

☐ Providing prompt feedback.

☐ Giving feedback that is relevant to the conversation.

☐ Changing the subject.

☐ Interrupting by waving your arms or stamping your feet.

☐ Using appropriate eye contact.

☐ Combining verbal and non-verbal (body language) feedback for more complete communication.

☐ Staring blankly.

☐ Asking a question for clarification.

☐ Mumbling.

Add you own responsible responses below:

SECTION III:
YOUR LISTENING STYLE—
A BARRIER OR A BRIDGE?

Listening style reflects the attitude and behavior of the listener. It is how an individual responds when listening. Your listening style can be a *bridge* or a *barrier* to good communication. Listeners can avoid the barriers of listening by being aware of what the pitfalls are, and knowing how to avoid them.

Following are some descriptions of listening styles. Answer the questions following each description which will help these "characters" improve their listening styles.

VACANT VINCENT

The most difficult person to communicate with is a daydreamer. Meet Vacant Vincent. You will recognize him by the far-away look in his eyes. Vincent is like a social butterfly who dips in and out of conversations picking up bits and pieces of information. He is physically present but "not really there". Vincent is easily distracted, and often changes the subject without warning. Sometimes he slouches as if he is tired. He plays with his tie or impatiently taps his pencil on the desk. The best way to get Vincent's attention is to talk about *his* interests.

How can Vincent become a better listener? Following is a list of listening behaviors. Check any that would help Vincent improve his communication skills.

1. ____ Sitting in a listening position
2. ____ Making eye contact
3. ____ Controlling distractions
4. ____ Playing with his computer

5. ____ Fidgeting
6. ____ Sticking to the subject
7. ____ Taking an interest in other people
8. ____ Losing his temper

Answers: 1, 2, 3, 6, 7.

The Business of Listening

BARRIERS TO COMMUNICATION (Continued)

CRITICAL CARRIE

Critical listening is important in business, especially when problems need to be resolved, but some listeners listen only to find fault. Critical Carrie listens to get all the facts, but is so critical of each item that she often misses "the big picture." Carrie frowns or rolls her eyes in disbelief as she listens to elements of a problem. Her questions for clarification are demanding and make her co-workers feel cornered. Critical Carrie is an incessant note taker, so her eye contact is limited. She finds little time for small talk. Her friends wish she would "lighten up" and not take things so seriously.

What would help Carrie communicate more effectively? Following is a list of listening behaviors. Check any that would help Carrie improve her listening style.

1. ____ Building rapport with "small talk"
2. ____ Listening for the "big picture"
3. ____ Taking more notes
4. ____ Becoming a better friend to herself
5. ____ Discrediting the speaker
6. ____ Determining the purpose of the discussion
7. ____ Developing patience
8. ____ Jumping to conclusions

Answers: 1, 2, 4, 6, 7.

COMPLIANT CURTIS

Compliant listening is a passive behavior that does not allow the speaker to understand the real feelings or opinions of the listener. Listeners such as Compliant Curtis listen much more than they talk. Often they are shy. They want to please others and keep communications pleasant. Compulsive talkers often seek out listeners like Compliant Curtis, because they need people with the patience to listen to them. Unfortunately, when Curtis speaks he usually keeps his *real* opinions to himself for fear of criticism. Sometimes he fakes attention as he silently thinks his private thoughts. In meetings Curtis nods his head approvingly, but adds little to the discussion. You will recognize Compliant Curtis by such phrases as ''That's nice,'' or ''I see your point.''

How can Curtis become a more involved listener? Check any of the following listening behaviors that would help him improve his listening style.

1. ____ Voicing his opinions
2. ____ Working to develop positive assertiveness*
3. ____ Daydreaming
4. ____ Asking questions
5. ____ Listening more intently
6. ____ Mentally finishing other people's sentences
7. ____ Speaking with conviction
8. ____ Avoiding eye contact

---

*For an excellent self-study book on this topic see page 67, *Developing Positive Assertiveness*.

Answers: 1, 2, 4, 6, 7.

BRIDGES TO COMMUNICATION

"Active" listening is the bridge to good communication. It is committed listening based on good habits and self control. Good listening is purposeful and productive because it allows the listener and the speaker to reach understanding. Following are descriptions of active listening styles that create positive communication.

ARLO ACTIVE

Arlo Active, a skilled training director, is an involved listener. He is "present" and participative and assumes responsibility for the success of communications in his department. In meetings and discussions Arlo requires discipline and relevance from his subordinates and bridges gaps in understanding by asking questions for clarification. Individuals in his department appreciate Arlo's clear verbal *and* non-verbal responses and focused eye contact. Arlo tries to see the other person's point of view and refrains from evaluating information too quickly. As an active listener, Arlo listens not only to the *content* of employees' statements, but also to their *intent*.

BRIDGES TO COMMUNICATION (Continued)

LISETTE LISTENER

Lisette Listener, a successful real estate agent, credits her success to active listening. When interviewing potential clients, Lisette listens carefully to their requirements for a home. She pays close attention to where they want to live, the desired style of house and the value they place on schools and services. She asks many questions for clarification. She then "feeds back" what she hears to be sure she is accurate in her interpretation. By the end of a busy "listening" day Lisette often feels as tired as if she had built a house, rather than sold one. She realizes that active listening is hard work but knows her results are measured clearly by her commissions, her satisfied new home owners, and new friends she makes because she helped them with a major decision.

Lisette Listener

BARRIERS AND BRIDGES
TO COMMUNICATION (Continued)

What other listening styles (positive and negative) can you think of?

Listening Styles	Style	Attitude Conveyed	Verbal or Non-verbal Behavior
Positive			
Negative			

SECTION IV:
HOW WELL DO YOU LISTEN?

A LISTENING ATTITUDE: YOUR KEY TO SUCCESS

What kind of a listener are you? Conscientious? Rushed? Thoughtful? Interruptive? This section provides you with some methods for self-evaluation as a listener. What is your listening style? How well does it contribute to your overall success in business? In your personal life?

Most people believe they are effective listeners. However, as previously noted, research indicates that on average we are effective and listen at only a 25% efficiency level. Much of the time we *think* we are listening. We seem to believe because we have ears we are listening. This is like believing that because we have eyes we can read. Undiagnosed bad habits such as interrupting, allowing ourselves to be distracted, jumping to conclusions, daydreaming or giving in to boredom prevent us from becoming the kind of listeners we think we are. The only way for us to progress is to make some conscious changes.

Change begins with an honest self-evaluation of our strengths *and* weaknesses. The exercises in this section will allow you to evaluate your listening style and plan a strategy for change.

Practicing the exercises in this section will make you a better listener. First, identify your listening problems and decide which changes you want to make. To be effective, plan positive action steps, and then practice specific listening skills at every opportunity. This will dramatically improve your ability to listen more effectively. Turn the page so you can begin to identify, plan and practice skills to improve your listening effectiveness.

A LISTENING ATTITUDE: YOUR KEY TO SUCCESS

Listening skill development is an ongoing process. Good listening is a key to success in any business environment. Discovering your attitude about listening is an important first step toward successful listening. Attitudes determine our behaviors. To discover your listening attitudes, complete the following exercise. If a statement describes your listening attitude or behavior check ''Yes,'' if not, check ''No.'' Be toughminded.

LISTENING ATTITUDES AND BEHAVIORS

	YES	NO
1. I am interested in many subjects and do not knowingly tune out dry-sounding information.	☑	☐
2. I listen carefully for a speaker's main ideas and supporting points.	☐	☑
3. I take notes during meetings to record key points.	☐	☑
4. I am not easily distracted.	☐	☑
5. I keep my emotions under control.	☐	☐
6. I concentrate carefully and do not fake attention.	☐	☐
7. I wait for the speaker to finish before finally evaluating the message.	☐	☐
8. I respond appropriately with a smile, a nod, or a word of acknowledgement, as a speaker is talking.	☐	☐
9. I am aware of mannerisms that may distract a speaker and keep mine under control.	☐	☐
10. I understand my biases and control them when I am listening.	☐	☐

LISTENING ATTITUDES AND BEHAVIORS (Continued)

	YES	NO
11. I refrain from constantly interrupting.	☐	☐
12. I value eye contact and maintain it most of the time.	☐	☐
13. I often restate or paraphrase what the speaker said to make sure I have the correct meaning.	☐	☐
14. I listen for the speaker's emotional meaning as well as subject matter content.	☐	☐
15. I ask questions for clarification.	☐	☐
16. I do not finish other people's sentences unless asked to do so.	☐	☐
17. When listening on the telephone one hand is kept free to take notes.	☐	☐
18. I attempt to set aside my ego and focus on the speaker rather than on myself.	☐	☐
19. I am careful to judge the message rather than the speaker.	☐	☐
20. I am a patient listener most of the time.	☐	☐

The following scale will help you interpret your present listening skill level based on your current attitudes and behaviors.

1-5 "No" answers	You are an excellent listener. Keep it up!
6-10 "No" answers	You are a good listener, but can improve.
11-15 "No" answers	Through practice you can become a much more effective listener in your business and personal relationships.
16-20 "No" answers	Listen up!

PERSONAL LISTENING INVENTORY

The Personal Listening Inventory on the facing page will help you rate yourself as a listener. An interpretation of results follows this inventory. When you have completed it you will have a better insight into:

How much time you spend listening;

How you rate yourself as a listener;

How you think others rate you as a listener;

How you rate others as listeners.

PERSONAL LISTENING INVENTORY

1. On a scale of 1-10 (with 10 being highest), how committed are you to improving your listening? ____

2. On average, what percentage of each business day do you spend listening? ____

3. On a scale of 1-10 (with 10 being highest), how would you rate yourself as a listener? ____

4. On a scale of 1-10, how would you rate the best listener you know? ____

5. On a scale of 1-10, how would you rate the worst listener you know? ____

6. On a scale of 1-10 (with 10 being highest), how would the following people (where appropriate) rate you as a listener?

Manager ____   Spouse/Lover ____

Subordinate ____   Child(ren) ____

Close colleague ____   Best friend ____

For the author's interpretation of the Personal Listening Inventory see the next page.

PERSONAL LISTENING INVENTORY— AUTHOR RESPONSES

The following interpretation of the Personal Listening Inventory you took on page 33 will help you compare your results with those of others.

1. We need to become committed to becoming better listeners, because **listening is hard work.** It requires patience, persistence and a plan for improvement. Casual involvement and genuine commitment are not the same thing. Suppose you had ham and eggs for breakfast. The chicken was involved in the meal, but the pig was committed. What is your commitment to your listening improvement?

2. According to experts we spend approximately 80% of each business day communicating. Of that time, 45% is spent listening, 30% speaking, 16% reading and 9% writing. A manager may spend up to 60% of each business day listening.

3. Most people listen at about 50% efficiency during the first part of an oral communication. In other words, if tested immediately on what they just heard they would accurately remember 50%. However, the efficiency rate drops quickly after the initial statements. Most people average a 25% efficiency rate overall.

4. Best listeners are usually rated as 8, 9 or 10. This is higher than most individuals rate themselves. The best listeners are often mentors, role models or professional counselors.

5. Worst listeners are usually rated at 0 - 4. This score is much lower than most people rate themselves. ''Worst listeners'' are often related to us, probably because we save our worst behaviors for the people closest to us.

6. It is not unusual to discover that our best friends rate us highest and our family lowest. Subordinates and colleagues rank us about the same as we rank ourselves. Bosses usually rank us higher than we rank ourselves because we listen (or pretend to) better to them than to others. In other words, we are more attentive when there is a direct payoff or penalty.

YOUR LISTENING QUALITIES: AN AWARENESS EXERCISE

1. List five of your best listening qualities, such as, patience, good eye contact, not jumping to conclusions, asking for clarification, etc., and rank them 1-5, with one (1) being your best quality.

    1.

    2.

    3.

    4.

    5.

2. List three listening qualities that you don't have now but would like to have.

    1.

    2.

    3.

3. List five of your worst listening qualities, such as impatience, poor eye contact, jumping to conclusions, not asking for clarification, etc., and rank them, with one (1) being the worst, etc.

    1.

    2.

    3.

    4.

    5.

4. List three listening qualities of poor listeners you know that you would like to avoid. Make a commitment to be more patient with those people, and not fall into those behaviors yourself.

    1.

    2.

    3.

Now turn to the next page to see how to eliminate bad listening habits and replace them with good ones.

HOW TO STOMP BAD LISTENING HABITS

1. **Catch yourself in the act.** Recognition is the first step for preventive maintenance. By listing the listening habits you want to eliminate on the previous page, you should be able to more readily recognize them. By monitoring your listening behavior you can catch yourself when you fall into an undesirable behavior, then take steps toward positive change.

2. **Fight the habit.** Don't tolerate what you want to eliminate from your listening style. Stomp it. Drop it. Change your ways! Like a smoker kicking the habit, cold turkey is the best way. Don't wait until next time to do things differently. Admit your behavior (i.e., "I just interrupted you. I'm sorry, please go on with what you were saying.") This is a way of catching yourself in the act and acknowledging your bad habit.

3. **Substitute the old habit with a new habit.** Memorize the list of new habits you want to develop. If you are chronically impatient, find a way to learn patience. For example, think about how you appreciate other people's patience when you are trying to explain something, then act the way you were treated. Visualize yourself as being patient (or not interrupting, or listening without daydreaming, etc.) Look for the value in the new behavior you select and trust yourself to do it.

4. **Acknowledge your success.** When you successfully substitute an improved listening behavior, give yourself a reward—a pat on the back. Put five dollars toward a vacation fund, or a star in your listening diary. Say to yourself "I did it!" Tell someone to see if they praise you; or better yet, tell someone you know *will* praise you.

SECTION V:
TEN TIPS FOR TIP-TOP LISTENING

Listening is both a behavior and a skill. Our behavior is the evidence of our ability to apply a skill. To improve our listening skills we need to consciously practice the ten tips in this section. A good driver does more than simply avoid accidents and a good listener does more than simply pay attention.

The following tips will help you "listen louder". Consciously select those you wish to work on and then establish a list of listening priorities. The Summary Section of this book contains a Personal Action Plan. Here you will be asked to list the listening skills you want to improve, developing some goals and establishing a plan to meet those goals.

Because business is a place where you need to listen most of the time, you will have plenty of opportunity to practice. Mentally condition yourself to make every encounter, from your first phone call to the last meeting of your business day, an opportunity to practice improved listening. Be practical and select the tips that will help you the most.

TEN TIPS FOR TIP-TOP LISTENING

TIP 1

Take notes. Good listeners are note-takers. They realize that minds are imprecise and memory is imperfect. Note-taking will help you identify unorganized speakers, help you locate the key points, and identify supporting data. The following suggestions can help you improve your note-taking skills.*

Be prepared. Carry a small note pad and a pen at all times. (Some people prefer to carry a small tape recorder.) Use the pad or tape recorder regularly to record any thoughts or ideas you want to remember. Note the source (speaker), situation, and time. (In selected situations you should ask permission before taking notes or recording what is said. Use good judgement).

Get it down. Don't take time to be overly neat. If necessary you can recopy your notes later. Write just clearly enough so you remember what you wrote and why you wrote it.

Don't try to write everything. Avoid complete sentences. Write nouns that create visual pictures. Use active verbs. Develop and use your own shorthand including symbols, pictures, punctuation and abbreviations (i.e., Suzie Hilgeman, lnch w/HP client, Fri. 11:30 @ JoJo's).

TIP 2

Listen now, report later. You can improve your listening significantly by planning to report what you heard to someone later. (Taking notes will increase your effectiveness even more.) Think of a co-worker or friend who would benefit from or enjoy the information you're listening to and plan to tell him/her what you've heard. Your listening then takes on the added dimension of a rehearsal.

CASE STUDY

*For an excellent review of note taking strategies, order "Study Skills Strategies, Your Guide to Critical Thinking", using the form on page 67.

TEN TIPS FOR TIP-TOP LISTENING (Continued)

CASE STUDY

Ray is the sales manager for a large manufacturing company in Seattle. Recently his company has received some customer complaints about one of their important new products. Ray quickly acted to set up a hotline and requested that all complaints be referred to him immediately.

By listening carefully to complaints from the customers, Ray was able to identify three specific manufacturing problems. He did not know personally how to solve the problems, but by responding quickly and listening carefully he assured his customers that action would be taken and the problems would be resolved. Because Ray showed concern by listening carefully, the customers agreed to support the product until a solution was found. They approved the time Ray estimated would be required to make the changes.

Ray took the information he received through listening to the manufacturing manager and carefully reported his findings. The manufacturing manager was upset by the magnitude of the problems, but grateful for the feedback. The manufacturing manager and his staff were able to make several adjustments to the manufacturing process which not only solved the problem, but actually improved the product.

HOW WOULD YOU RATE RAY AS A LISTENER?

_____ Excellent   _____ Good   _____ Average   _____ Fair   _____ Poor

TEN TIPS FOR TIP-TOP LISTENING (Continued)

TIP 3	**Learn to want to listen.** To be good listeners we must be willing to give up a preoccupation with ourselves. Simply put, we must learn to *want* to listen. The following memory device describes the skills and attitudes we need to insure our listening success:

TO BE A GOOD LISTENER, USE YOUR *DISC* DRIVE

D = Desire.   From a desire to listen comes commitment. A committed athlete does not play half of each game. We must *want* to learn to listen to be a truly effective communicator.

I = Interest   According to G. K. Chesterton, there is no such thing as an uninteresting topic, there are just uninterested people. We must learn to develop an interest in either the person and/or the topic in order to be a good listener.

S = Self Discipline   We must learn self-discipline in order to eliminate distractions, understand the speaker's key points, overcome boredom, interpret voice inflection and tone, understand non-verbal cues and comprehend the main idea. Next time you are in a listening situation, pay attention to how well you control your listening habits. Monitoring your listening behavior is essential to taking positive action later.

C = Concentration   Concentration is focused mental energy. Think of concentration as your salary. If you are like most people, your salary is a limited resource that must be spent carefully. If you do not concentrate on your income versus your expenses you will soon have trouble. Lack of concentration in listening is no different.

As products of the "TV generation" most of us concentrate intensely for only a few moments at a time. Try flipping on the TV to see how long you can concentrate before your mind wanders. If you are like most people you will probably focus for only a few seconds.

TEN TIPS FOR TIP-TOP LISTENING (Continued)

LISTENING LAB

Complete the following exercise to identify reasons you do not always concentrate:

CONCENTRATION CHECKLIST

Rate the following which apply to you using a scale from 0-3, with 0 being no problem; 1 being a minor problem; 2 being somewhat of a problem; and 3 being a major problem. Total your score and compare it to the box at the end of the exercise.

1. I'm in a hurry _____

2. I become distracted by what is going on around me _____

3. I'm self-conscious _____

4. I'm bored _____

5. I'm thinking about what I'm going to say next _____

6. I'm in surroundings that are "out of my comfort zone" _____

7. I already know what the speaker is going to say _____

8. I'm used to having things repeated _____

9. I'm on mental overload most of the time _____

10. I'm not responsible for the information given _____

11. I'm tired _____

12. I'm confused by the topic or the speaker _____

13. I'm daydreaming _____

0-5	You have excellent concentration skills.
6-10	This book should help improve your concentration skills.
11 or more	You need help putting into practice a specific action plan to improve concentration skills.

TEN TIPS FOR TIP-TOP LISTENING (Continued)

TIP 3 **CON'T**	To improve your concentration develop an opportunistic attitude. Ask yourself these questions:

• What's in it for me?

• What can I learn or pass along to a co-worker?

• How can I use this information?

Concentration improves when you develop mental pictures of what the speaker is saying. If Joe calls to say that he will have the Wilson report on your desk by 2:30 p.m. on Friday, visualize Joe placing the report on your desk. Notice how Joe is dressed. Image the word WILSON in bold letters on the cover of the report. See in your mind a clock that reads 2:30 p.m. next to your desk calendar turned to Friday. By visualizing what you want to remember, you create ''dwell time'' for your mind to encode the information into your long term memory.

To be a good listener we must use our *DISC* Drive. Just as a disc drive runs the computer, so our personal *DISC* Drive controls our attitudes, skills and behaviors in listening situations.

TIP 4	**Be Present.** Like it or not, we always choose whether and how well we are going to listen. When we choose not to listen, our minds are on vacation and we do not interpret, evaluate or respond appropriately to the speaker and the message. Only when we choose to ''be present'' are we focused on the speaker and the message.

Our number one alternative to being present is daydreaming. Daydreaming is a comfortable private escape. It normally doesn't disturb anyone and often others don't realize we're doing it. Daydreaming is what we elect to do when we choose not to be present.

Daydreaming is the single greatest barrier to active listening. To be present and listen effectively, we must recognize our mental vacations, put them aside and bring ourselves back to the subject at hand. The exercise on the facing page will help you recognize your **''DQ'' (Daydream Quotient)** and suggest steps to take in order to be present in your listening.

TEN TIPS FOR TIP-TOP LISTENING (Continued)

LISTENING LAB

YOUR "DQ" (DAYDREAM QUOTIENT)

In the following exercise take a piece of paper and jot down any time you daydream as you read the rest of this book. If your mind wanders, jot down where it went and what you were thinking about, then quickly return your attention to your reading. Reading and listening are similar in that they both allow opportunities for daydreaming. Notice any tendency you may have to let your mind wander as you read, and write it down in the space below. When you complete **The Business of Listening,** review your "DQ" to see if there are repeated subjects or patterns in your daydreams. If so, they may be matters for conscious attention and action.

WE ALL DAYDREAM

We all daydream. Many of us as much as 50% of the time. Next time you are in a listening situation check your DQ to notice how often you mentally wander off while the speaker is talking. If you "wander" at least once per minute, chances are you need more concentration and self discipline in your listening.

Effective listeners focus on the speaker and listen hard for the content of the message. They avoid the embarrassment of being caught daydreaming. While we are never tested on our daydreams, we can, at any time, be tested on the content of the message.

TEN TIPS FOR TIP-TOP LISTENING (Continued)

TIP 5

Anticipate excellence. In the film *"Brain Power"*, John Houseman presents a powerful story about a group of normal men who checked themselves into a mental hospital. Each had invented a different story explaining why he was crazy. All studied and displayed classic textbook symptoms of the disease. Once inside the hospital they began to tell the truth, but no one believed them. Only after great difficulty and with outside verification were they released from the hospital.

Expectations play a powerful role in our lives. How often have we avoided a co-worker because we didn't want to spend time listening to small talk. Other times we may have made up an excuse to miss a speaker we expected to be boring.

By giving others a chance to speak intelligently and by anticipating excellence from them, we can help them become successful. As humans we have a deep and unending need to be heard and understood. When we set aside our needs and truly listen, people will drop their pretenses and speak to us in a more mature and connected manner.

Listeners can help speakers by

- Asking questions
- Showing interest
- Expressing concern
- Paying attention

PEOPLE DO THEIR BEST WHEN THEY KNOW

SOMEONE IS LISTENING.

THE PIONEER'S STORY

The following story is about some pioneers in covered wagons who crossed into the new Oregon Territory. They stopped to rest at a small settlement and the wagon master spoke to an old man sunning himself in front of the General Store.

"Say, Old Timer, what kind of people have settled out here?"

"What kind of people were they where you came from?" asked the old man.

"Well, they were mean, full of mischief and small minded. That's why we left," said the wagon master.

"Sorry to say, young feller, but that's the kind of folks you'll find out here," replied the old man.

Later in the week another team of wagons pulled into town for supplies. This wagon master also stopped in front of the general store and saw the same old man sunning on the steps.

"Say, Old Timer, what kind of people have settled out here?"

"What kind of people were they where you came from?", asked the old man again.

"The people we left behind were kind, decent people and they were generous. When we left they gave us supplies and helped us load our wagons. We all miss them very much," sighed the wagon master.

"Well, my fiend, you've come to the right place, because those are the kind of people you're going to find out here," replied the old man with a kindly smile.

We get what we expect! Anticipate excellence, and it will happen a lot more often than if we assume otherwise.

TEN TIPS FOR TIP-TOP LISTENING (Continued)

TIP 6

Become a "Whole Body" Listener. To be effective listeners we must involve our whole body. Not only are our ears tuned in, but so are our eyes, our mind (the intellect), our bodies and hearts. Good listeners give both non-verbal and verbal signals that they are listening.

A "whole body" listener listens actively by:
- Conveying a positive encouraging attitude
- Sitting in an attentive posture (facing the speaker)
- Remaining alert, but comfortable.
- Nodding in acknowledgement of the speaker's words
- Making good eye contact
- Ignoring or eliminating distractions
- Tuning in to the speaker's feelings
- Looking like a listener

If you are in total rapport you will naturally match the speaker's physical movements, tone of voice, vocabulary and breathing patterns. Good listeners are in sensory balance with the speaker.

According to Albert Mehrabian, a noted expert in human behavior, our communication is 55% Non-verbal, 38% Inflection and tone and only 7% Words.

If Mehrabian is correct, then most of the message is *seen* and *sensed,* and the words are far less important than the non-verbal cues and tone of voice.

Think about your personal mannerisms and behaviors. Do you have any of the following habits that would distract or confuse a speaker?
- Fidgeting
- Blinking
- Biting your lip
- Frowning deeply
- Playing with your hair, tie or jewelry
- Looking at your watch
- etc.

Stop for a moment and think about these behaviors. Would they distract you if you were the one speaking? If your answer is yes, you need to find a way to modify your behavior. Try the suggestions on the facing page.

TEN TIPS FOR TIP-TOP LISTENING (Continued)

LISTENING LAB

1. Body Check Exercise

Briefly describe your non-verbal listening responses with two people you know. Make one a person you enjoy and the other a person you don't. Are your responses different? If so, how? If you want to change any of your non-verbal responses to either person use the *Change* line to state your improvement goal.

Person #1 _____

Response	*Description*	*Change*

Posture
Eye Contact
Facial Expression
Mannerisms
General Attitude
Voice (verbal response)

Person #2 _____

Response	*Description*	*Change*

Posture
Eye Contact
Facial Expression
Mannerisms
General Attitude
Voice (verbal response)

2. Non-Verbal Encouragement Exercise

List five things you can do non-verbally to encourage a speaker.

1.

2.

3.

4.

5.

TEN TIPS FOR TIP-TOP LISTENING (Continued)

TIP 7

Build Rapport by Pacing the Speaker.
Pacing is a method listeners use to build rapport with a speaker by imitating or mirroring his or her behaviors. These include gestures, breathing, voice rate, vocabulary, favorite phrases and facial expressions. Of course if we imitate too closely we will be accused of mimicking and our attempts to build rapport will be lost. When pacing, a good listener focuses on who the speaker is and what he or she is saying. The listener then makes a conscious effort to overcome the differences between them. The sooner the speaker and listener find common ground, the sooner they can communicate at a comfortable level. From that point, their opportunity for mutual understanding will be greater.

As a listener, you can pace a speaker in any of the following ways:

1. **Match your voice rate to theirs.** Speed up or slow down as necessary.

2. **Change your voice volume to match theirs.**

3. **Notice and use some of the same words and phrases as the speaker.**

4. **Approximate the speaker's gestures.** Sit forward or back, hands on or off the desk, etc. (Do not be too obvious or you will be noticed. *Approximate* the gestures.)

5. **Breathe at about the same rate, without being too obvious.** (If the speaker is a Type A and breathes very fast be careful not to hyperventilate.)

CHERYL'S STORY

Cheryl was preparing to give a technical speech before a large important audience. She arrived early at the meeting room to test her slides and adapt to the circumstances of the room. When she turned on the rented projector, the bulb in the machine suddenly burned out. Cheryl looked in the projector case but could not find a replacement. Frantically Cherly searched the building for a maintenance person. She found the maintenance supervisor on the next floor, ambling slowly down the hall. She rushed to the supervisor, explaining her dilemma in a rapid staccato voice which displayed an obvious urgency.

Bill, the supervisor was low keyed. While Cheryl churned like a buzz saw, Bill spoke no faster than a snail on Valium. Cheryl felt she could count to ten between each of Bill's words. "I'd - like - to - help - you, - but - I don't - have - a - key - to - the - supply - closet," Bill said in a low slow patient monotone. Cheryl continued to buzz and Bill continued to dawdle for several more minutes.

Suddenly Cheryl remembered something she had read about pacing a speaker and she decided to give it a try. Gradually she began to slow her speech to match Bill's rate. It was painful for Cheryl to talk so slowly, but Bill became more responsive and more helpful as she became less frantic.

Within minutes Bill remembered someone who had a key and volunteered to find the bulb she needed. Cheryl couldn't be sure the pacing made the difference, but within fifteen minutes she had the replacement bulb. Bill flashed her a big slow smile as he handed her the bulb, along with a spare in case the replacement burned out. Cheryl thanked him s-l-o-w-l-y, and smiled back. She had found a new friend.

BYRON'S STORY

Byron was an independent sales representative for a refrigeration company in Alaska. Because of his large territory Byron made most of his contacts by telephone. Byron had heard of pacing from a friend and decided to try it in his cold calls and follow-up over the phone.

When he called potential customers he listened very carefully to *what* they said and *how* they said it. Then as he spoke, he paced their voices, speed, inflection and vocabulary. With no other variables in his experiment other than pacing, Byron was able to increase his refrigeration equipment sales by 30% over the previous quarter.

TEN TIPS FOR TIP-TOP LISTENING (Continued)

LISTENING LAB

Pacing the Speaker

To develop an ability to pace effectively, follow these guidelines in the suggested sequence:

1. Practice pacing with a friend. Tell him or her what you are doing first. Have your friend tell you a funny story or describe an interesting place to visit and use varied gestures and facial expressions. Mirror each action and expression to get the feeling for the pacing activity. Afterwards discuss how successful you were and solicit suggestions for improvement.

2. Next, practice pacing on a friend or family member in a no-risk situation. Try to remain undetected.

3. Finally, practice on a colleague choosing one or two characteristics to mirror. Be natural and sincere. As you pace and observe, exhibit an attitude of wanting to build rapport.

Rapport is the ultimate tool in producing positive results with others. In business, dealing effectively with people is essential. Rapport can help us achieve success, and we build rapport by listening actively and acting on what we learn.

THE THREE KEYS TO PACING

1 Focused observation

2 Complete flexibility

3 Tuned in listening

TEN TIPS FOR TIP-TOP LISTENING (Continued)

TIP 8	**Control Your Emotional ''Hotbuttons''.** Words, issues, situations, and/or personalities trigger us emotionally. When these issues trigger our emotional ''hotbuttons'' a verbal message will become distorted (either positively or negatively). Because issues are emotional they create barriers to effective listening. When our ''hotbuttons'' are activated, we tune out, distort or prejudge these emotionally charged messages. The Three-Step method on the next page can help you identify your listening hotbuttons.

IDENTIFY YOUR EMOTIONAL "HOTBUTTONS"

TEN TIPS FOR TIP-TOP LISTENING (Continued)

LISTENING LAB

Identifying Emotional "Hotbuttons"

Step I Following are some listening situations and phrases that may cause you to be emotional. Check those that are "hotbuttons" for you as a listener, and add others that strongly affect you, positively or negatively.

_____ "You never/always..."

_____ Know-it-all attitudes

_____ Individuals who smoke cigarettes or cigars while talking to you

_____ "Shut up!"

_____ Bigots

_____ Bad grammar

_____ "You never listen."

_____ Pushy individuals

_____ Whining

_____ "What you should do is..."

Others:

_____

_____

_____

TEN TIPS FOR TIP-TOP LISTENING (Continued)

Step II   Read through the list again and cross out any "hotbutton" issues you are willing to give up, in other words, those you can forget, and not let them bother you any more. Chances are you will not cross many items off your list. This step demonstrates that it is difficult to give up habitual ways of responding to emotional situations.

Step III   Check the responses (triggers) on the following list that describe your physical reactions to emotional issues:

____ Heartbeat increases.

____ Hands feel sweaty.

____ Voice shakes.

____ Chest tightens.

Others: ____

____

____

Emotional "hotbuttons" are intense complex feelings that affect everyone. Each may initiate a different emotional reaction, but our physical responses are similar. If you cannot eliminate your emotional "hotbuttons", the best alternative is to develop acceptable responses. The triggers (listed above) warn you that emotions are taking over. When emotional levels go up, objectivity comes down. Problems are never satisfactorily resolved at an emotional level.

To control emotional hotbuttons we must identify what triggers us, understand our responses, and develop behaviors which allow us to listen more carefully and objectively.

TEN TIPS FOR TIP-TOP LISTENING (Continued)

Ten Steps for Controlling Emotional "Hotbuttons"

Following is a list of coping skills for preventive maintenance when your hotbutton is activated by someone's anger or frustration.

1. **Listen attentively without interrupting.** Take several deep breaths to help you control your physical reactions.

2. **Make a *conscious* choice about your response.** You can get angry, try to solve the problem, or ignore it. (Trying to solve the problem is the best way to keep it from happening again.)

3. **Acknowledge the other person's feelings.** Make it okay for them to feel the way they do.

4. **Ask objective questions for clarification.** Open ended questions are useful.

5. **Try to see the other person's point of view.** Agree where you can and feed back what you are hearing.

6. **Stick to the subject.** Define your problem and don't let other issues interfere.

7. **Be patient.** Problems don't always have immediate solutions. Be patient with the other person—and yourself.

8. **Express your point of view.** Don't force proof. Present your evidence without backing them into a corner.

9. **Explain why.** A reasonable explanation can often take the sting out of an emotional issue.

10. **Work out a "win-win" plan.** Make sure your solution is fair and workable for both (or all) of the people involved.

For additional suggestions for changing behavior refer to "The Joy of Small Change" on page 10.

TEN TIPS FOR TIP-TOP LISTENING (Continued)

LISTENING LAB

Preventive Maintenance for Emotional "Hotbuttons"

In the first column below list three people who affect you emotionally when you listen to them. Next write down the "hotbutton" issue that activates your reaction. Finally, develop a preventive maintenance plan to control or modify your emotional reaction.

Person	"Hotbutton"	Preventive Maintenance Plan

1.

2.

3.

TEN TIPS FOR TIP-TOP LISTENING (Continued)

<table>
<tr><td>

TIP 9

</td><td>

Control Distractions. Comedy star, George Carlin, once asked, ''Aren't you glad the phone wasn't invented by Alexander Graham Siren?'' A telephone is one of the biggest distractions to listening in a business environment, because unseen others choose when the phone will ring.* If the phone were the only distraction we could probably learn to tolerate it. Every day we must deal with many internal, external, visual and auditory distractions.

</td></tr>
</table>

To be good listeners, we must control our responses to distractions or they will control us. Distractions affect our ability to listen well because of their *variety*, *novelty* or *intensity*. External distractions include the telephone, background noise, unfamiliarity with vocabulary, seating, lighting, etc. Internal distractions can be things such as headaches, hunger, fatigue, or a current emotional state, such as anxiety.

STEPHANIE'S STORY

Stephanie was putting the finishing touches on a major marketing project when a co-worker called to discuss a budget problem. Stephanie automatically grabbed the phone and answered while still assembling binders. Suddenly she realized her distraction and set the binders aside. She told her co-worker politely that she was just finishing a project with a tight deadline and asked if she could return the call in an hour when the project was completed so she could be a better listener. By handling the matter this way, Stephanie avoided being distracted. She let the caller know her desire to give the budget problem her full attention as soon as possible.

Life and work are full of distractions. Part of our professional responsibility is to manage our working environment. Although our working conditions will never be ideal, we can minimize distractions by taking action to improve our listening, which will help reduce communication failures.

---

*For an excellent book *Time Management on the Telephone,* see page 67.

TEN TIPS FOR TIP-TOP LISTENING (Continued)

LISTENING LAB

Overcoming Distractions

The following statements describe how people might handle various distractions. Check those items you do well.

☐ **Plan your listening.** Don't attempt important business in a restaurant. It's too noisy and you're interrupted frequently. Find a quiet room away from the phone for important meetings. Plan decision-making meetings during your high energy times of the day. Think about possible distractions and plan to avoid as many as you can.

☐ **Don't use distractions as a convenient excuse for not listening.** Overcome distractions with extra concentration and determination.

☐ **Identify what is causing a distraction and make adjustments.** Are you too near a noisy copier? (Can you move away from it?) Do you have a headache? (Have you taken an aspirin?) Are you hungry? (Can you eat an apple?) Are the lights too low or too high? (Can they be adjusted?) Is the phone a problem? (Could someone take your calls?) In other words, when you have identified the problem, you are one step closer to fixing it.

☐ **Ignore the distraction.** If you can't do anything about the distraction, tune it out by concentrating harder. Although you know the distraction is there, focus your attention on the speaker. Use self-discipline.

☐ **Call "time out" when you are too tired to listen.** Audial (hearing) fatigue is caused by constant noise such as fans humming or the drone of machinery or traffic. Intense concentration or physical exhaustion can also cause "ear exhaustion". Don't be shy about calling a halt when you have had enough noise.

<table>
<tr>
<td>

TIP 10

</td>
<td>

Listening is a Gift, Give Generously. Listening is a skill that anyone can learn, and it is also a gift that anyone can give. It is a gift of a person's time and attention. Listening is an acknowledgement of caring. Honest listening encourages a speaker to be creative and feel more accepted.

</td>
</tr>
</table>

TEN TIPS FOR TIP-TOP LISTENING (Continued)

According to author, Tom Peters, in his book, ''In Search of Excellence'' top executives have learned to be excellent listeners. They understand the importance of good listening. The best managers do far more than allow listening to happen. They realize that listening improves effectiveness, accomplishes more, and earns profits.

The gift of listening assumes the speaker has value, dignity and something to offer. We must listen every day in the business world. If in our listening we take the focus off of ourselves and encourage the speaker to express his/her ideas we extend a gift that will be repaid many times. Develop a listening attitude. The results are worth it.

CONSIDER A GIFT CERTIFICATE

A GIFT OF LISTENING

This certificate entitles you to one-half hour of my undivided attention. I will listen to you carefully and thoughtfully. I will not interrupt, and I'll only ask questions for clarification.

When would you like your gift?

_____

Listener

SECTION VI
SUMMARY: POINTS TO REMEMBER

Section I   Why Should You (or Anyone) Listen?

- Work and listening are inseparable.

- Lazy listening is a hidden cost of doing business.

- We listen for our own reasons.

- We can improve listening with desire, motivation and a plan for constructive change.

Section II   Four Key Elements of Listening: How to be a Good Listener

- Hear the message. Listen to both verbal and non-verbal information.

- Interpret the message. A good interpretation is a match-up of meaning between the speaker and the listener.

- Evaluate the message. The listener's opinion should be based on *all* available information. Ask questions.

- Respond to the message. Good listening means giving the speaker an appropriate response, verbally and/or non-verbally.

Section III   Your Listening Style—A Barrier or a Bridge?

- Behavior reflects attitude.

- How we look and act as listeners determines our listening style.

SUMMARY:
POINTS TO REMEMBER (Continued)

Section IV   How Well Do You Listen?

- Most people aren't good listeners.

- A good listener encourages positive results.

- We listen best when there is a payoff or a penalty.

- Personal listening awareness is the key to constructive change.

Section V   Ten Tips for Tip-Top Listening

- Take notes. They aid retention.

- Listen now, report later. Plan to tell someone what you heard, you will remember it better.

- Learn to want to listen. You must have Desire, Interest, Self-discipline and Concentration to be a good listener.

- Be present. Watch the tendency to daydream.

- Anticipate excellence. We get good information more often when we expect it.

- Become a "whole-body" listener. Listen with your ears, your eyes and your heart.

- Build rapport by pacing the speaker. Approximate the speaker's gestures, expressions and voice patterns to create comfortable communication.

- Control your emotional "hot-buttons". Knowing what makes you react emotionally is your key to preventive maintenance.

- Control distractions. Controlling internal and external distractions helps you manage your working environment more effectively.

- Give the gift of listening. Listening is a skill, and a gift. Give generously.

DEVELOP A PERSONAL ACTION PLAN

A definition of ACCOUNTABILITY is to be responsible for one's actions.

We all have good intentions. The thing that separates those who are successful from those who are not is how well these ''good intentions'' are carried out.

A voluntary action plan can convert your good intentions into actions.

The PERSONAL ACTION PLAN on the facing page is a good starting point if you are serious about improving your listening skills.

This action plan can be initiated the next time you are in the role of listener.

PERSONAL ACTION PLAN (Continued)

Think about the information you have read in this book. Review the exercises, questionnaires and case studies. What did you learn about listening? What did you learn about yourself as a listener? How can you improve your listening skills? Make a commitment to improving your listening in your business and personal life. Design a personal action plan to help you reach your goal.

The following guide may help you clarify your goals and outline actions to achieve them.

1. My current listening skills are effective in the following areas:

2. I need to improve my listening skills in the following areas:

3. I will implement an action plan for listening improvement in the following manner:

    A. My listening goals:

    B. My *plan* for reaching my goals:

    C. My timetable:

    (Refer to page 36 ''How to Stomp Bad Habits'' for reinforcement.)

4. The following person(s) will benefit from my improved listening skills:

5. They will benefit in the following ways:

KATHY'S STORY

On Kathy Green's thirtieth birthday she cautiously invited her parents to join the celebration with a few friends. Her mother had baked Kathy's favorite lemon cake and Kathy felt obligated. However, she was concerned about what the reaction of her friends might be to her parents. Kathy's father was hard-of-hearing and shouted when he spoke. Her mother in turn shouted at her father to tell him what other people were saying. Mrs. Green also talked constantly and changed the subject frequently. Almost any response from her listener would catapult Mrs. Green onto a new topic. Kathy had long since given up really listening to her mother. Kathy's behavior was cool and polite, but non-caring.

Kathy attended a company seminar on listening shortly before the celebration. She realized that although she listened effectively to co-workers, she had developed a habitual "unhearing" response to her mother.

At her birthday dinner, Kathy began to realize that her mother's behavior was a bid for attention. Mrs. Green was isolated from her husband by his hearing loss and from her only child, by Kathy's imposed distancing. It was true that her mother did not have good communication skills, but Kathy realized that her mother changed the topic in an attempt to be more interesting. The more she was rebuffed, the more she changed the subject.

Kathy made a decision following the night of her birthday to pay more attention to her mother. She focused her listening and developed a genuine interest in what her mother was saying. She worked hard to break old listening patterns and substitute new ones. First she noticed only small changes. Her mother began to stick to the subject longer as Kathy asked patient, relevant questions and listened to the answers. At times Kathy had to guide her mother back to the subject, but she was persistent in her resolve.

Kathy's Story (Continued)

After six months Kathy noticed that her mother was calmer and more connected when she spoke. She stopped talking as much and listened with interest as Kathy told her about a recent promotion. True, Mrs. Green still shouted at Mr. Green, but Kathy stopped hearing it as much. Thanks to a simple increase in listening effectiveness, Kathy was able to renew a loving relationship with her parents.

Kathy learned well the business of listening and we hope you are on your way to doing the same. Good Luck!

ABOUT THE FIFTY-MINUTE SERIES

''Fifty-Minute books are the best new publishing idea in years. They are clear, practical, concise and affordable — perfect for today's world.''

Leo Hauser
(Past President, ASTD)

What Is A Fifty-Minute Book?

—Fifty-Minute books are brief, soft-cover, ''self-study'' modules which cover a single concept. They are reasonably priced, and ideal for formal training programs, excellent for self-study and perfect for remote location training.

Why Are Fifty-Minute Books Unique?

—Because of their format and level. Designed to be ''read with a pencil,'' the basics of a subject can be quickly grasped and applied through a series of hands-on activities, exercises and cases.

How Many Fifty-Minute Books Are There?

—Those listed on the facing page at this time, however, additional titles are in development. For more information write to **Crisp Publications, Inc., 95 First Street, Los Altos, CA 94022.**

THE FIFTY-MINUTE SERIES

Quantity	Title	Code #	Price	Amount
	The Fifty-Minute Supervisor—*2nd Edition*	58-0	$6.95	
	Effective Performance Appraisals—*Revised*	11-4	$6.95	
	Successful Negotiation—*Revised*	09-2	$6.95	
	Quality Interviewing—*Revised*	13-0	$6.95	
	Team Building: An Exercise in Leadership—*Revised*	16-5	$6.95	
	Performance Contracts: The Key To Job Success—*Revised*	12-2	$6.95	
	Personal Time Management	22-X	$6.95	
	Effective Presentation Skills	24-6	$6.95	
	Better Business Writing	25-4	$6.95	
	Quality Customer Service	17-3	$6.95	
	Telephone Courtesy & Customer Service	18-1	$6.95	
	Restaurant Server's Guide To Quality Service—*Revised*	08-4	$6.95	
	Sales Training Basics—*Revised*	02-5	$6.95	
	Personal Counseling—*Revised*	14-9	$6.95	
	Balancing Home & Career	10-6	$6.95	
	Mental Fitness: A Guide To Emotional Health	15-7	$6.95	
	Attitude: Your Most Priceless Possession	21-1	$6.95	
	Preventing Job Burnout	23-8	$6.95	
	Successful Self-Management	26-2	$6.95	
	Personal Financial Fitness	20-3	$7.95	
	Job Performance and Chemical Dependency	27-0	$7.95	
	Career Discovery—*Revised*	07-6	$6.95	
	Study Skills Strategies—*Revised*	05-X	$6.95	
	I Got The Job!—*Revised*	59-9	$6.95	
	Effective Meetings Skills	33-5	$7.95	
	The Business of Listening	34-3	$6.95	
	Professional Sales Training	42-4	$7.95	
	Customer Satisfaction: The Other Half of Your Job	57-2	$7.95	
	Managing Disagreement Constructively	41-6	$7.95	
	Professional Excellence for Secretaries	52-1	$6.95	
	Starting A Small Business: A Resource Guide	44-0	$7.95	
	Developing Positive Assertiveness	38-6	$6.95	
	Writing Fitness-Practical Exercises for Better Business Writing	35-1	$7.95	
	An Honest Day's Work: Motivating Employees to Give Their Best	39-4	$6.95	
	Marketing Your Consulting & Professional Services	40-8	$7.95	
	Time Management On The Telephone	53-X	$6.95	
	Training Managers to Train	43-2	$7.95	
	New Employee Orientation	46-7	$6.95	
	The Art of Communicating: Achieving Impact in Business	45-9	$7.95	
	Technical Presentation Skills	55-6	$7.95	
	Plan B: Protecting Your Career from the Winds of Change	48-3	$7.95	
	A Guide To Affirmative Action	54-8	$7.95	
	Memory Skills in Business	56-4	$6.95	

(Continued on next page)

THE FIFTY-MINUTE SERIES
(Continued)

☐ Send volume discount information.

☐ Add my name to CPI's mailing list.

	Amount
Total (from other side)	
Shipping ($1.25 first book, $.50 per title thereafter)	
California Residents add 7% tax	
Total	

Ship to: _____

_____

_____

_____

Phone number: _____

Bill to: _____

_____

_____

P.O. # _____

**All orders except those with a P.O.# must be prepaid.
Call (415) 949-4888 for more information.**

NO POSTAGE
NECESSARY
IF MAILED
IN THE
UNITED STATES

BUSINESS REPLY
FIRST CLASS   PERMIT NO. 884   LOS ALTOS, CA

POSTAGE WILL BE PAID BY ADDRESSEE

Crisp Publications, Inc.
95 First Street
Los Altos, CA 94022

NOTES

NOTES

NOTES

NOTES